FIFE EDUCATION
COMMITTEE
KING'S ROAD P. SCHOOL
ROSYTH

Healthy
Skin

Wayne Jackman

Healthy Living

Healthy Teeth
Healthy Hair
Healthy Skin
Healthy Eyes
Healthy Hands and Feet
Healthy Eating

Words printed in **bold** are explained in the glossary

First Published in 1990 by
Wayland Publishers Limited
61 Western Road, Hove
East Sussex, BN3 1JD, England

© Copyright 1990 Wayland (Publishers) Ltd.

Consultant: Diana Bentley, Reading
Consultant, University of Reading
Editor: James Kerr

British Library Cataloguing in Publication Data
Jackman, Wayne
  Healthy skin.
  1. Man. Skin. Care
  I. Title
  646.726

  ISBN 1–85210–928–9

Typeset by N. Taylor, Wayland Publishers Limited
Printed and bound by Casterman S.A., Belgium

Contents

What is skin?

Look at these children. Just like you, their bodies are covered with skin. Skin can be many different colours: black, brown, white and other shades in between.

You can see from this diagram that skin is made up of two layers of **cells**. The top layer is called the epidermis.

This is a very thin layer of dead cells which constantly flake off. Because the cells are so small, you cannot see or feel them fall off. Below the epidermis is a thicker layer, called the dermis. This is a layer of living cells. They are gradually pushed to the surface as new cells grow underneath.

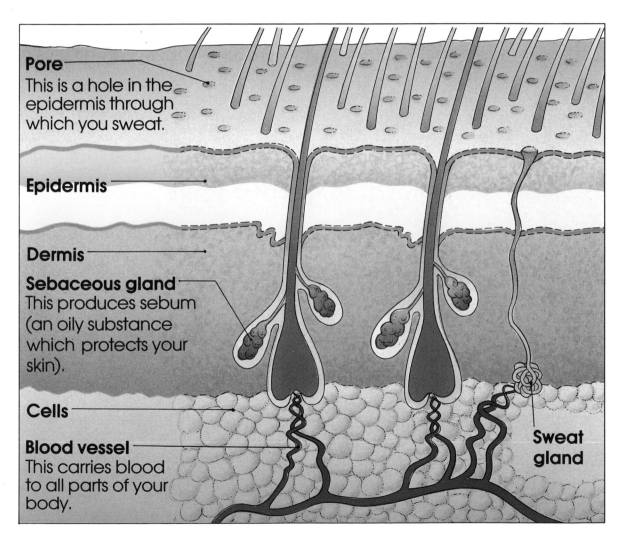

Pore
This is a hole in the epidermis through which you sweat.

Epidermis

Dermis

Sebaceous gland
This produces sebum (an oily substance which protects your skin).

Cells

Blood vessel
This carries blood to all parts of your body.

Sweat gland

Why healthy skin is important

Skin keeps important body fluids, like blood, inside your body, and keeps out germs and water. If you went swimming without your skin, water would get inside your body and you would end up as soggy as a wet sponge! Skin keeps your body at an even temperature. To do this, it allows you to sweat when you are hot and this 'cools' you down.

Skin also protects you from harmful rays of sunlight, and poisonous gases such as car exhaust fumes. Healthy skin is stretchy and **flexible**. It heals quickly if it is cut. **Nerve endings** in your skin allow you to feel heat, cold, pain and pressure.

Now you can see why it is so important for your skin to be fit and healthy.

Clean skin keeps us healthy

Your skin produces an oily substance called **sebum**. This helps to keep your skin stretchy, but also collects dust and dirt. Sweat leaves dirt on your skin too. Dirt can block up your **pores** and attract germs, both of which could give you spots or a **rash**. So it is very important to clean away the dirt by regular washing.

It is especially important to keep your hands clean. You could become ill if you put dirty fingers in your mouth. You might also spread germs to other people if your hands are dirty. Hands should always be washed after going to the toilet, and before a meal.

How to keep skin clean and healthy

In the morning, always wash your face and hands. It is a good idea to take a bath or shower before going to bed.

It is also a good idea to shower after swimming in the sea or a swimming-pool. This will wash away any **chlorine** or salt in the water.

10

Using a sponge or flannel helps to rub off dead skin cells and unblock your pores. Sometimes, a loofah – which is a rough sponge – is useful for a really thorough scrub, especially on your back.

Remember that flannels and towels can collect germs, and that using clean ones will stop infections from spreading.

How diet affects skin

A healthy diet will give you healthy skin. Too many oily, fatty foods such as fried eggs, hamburgers and chips can cause spots, especially in teenagers. Some people say that sweets, chocolate and fizzy pop may make your skin oily and spotty.

For healthy, clear skin, eat plenty of fresh fruit, green vegetables, milk, eggs, potatoes, carrots and cereals.

These contain the **vitamins** your body needs, including vitamins C and D. Without enough vitamins, your skin can look pale and be more easily bruised and scraped. Sometimes a lack of vitamin C can cause small **blood vessels** in your skin to break. This makes the skin look red and blotchy.

In hot weather your skin can sweat out over two litres of water every day! So drink plenty of liquids to replace it.

Cuts, scratches and bruises

If you cut or scratch yourself, your skin immediately begins to heal if it is healthy. Your blood forms a **clot** which hardens into a scab. Then, over a short period of time, the skin underneath the scab grows new cells to mend the **wound**.

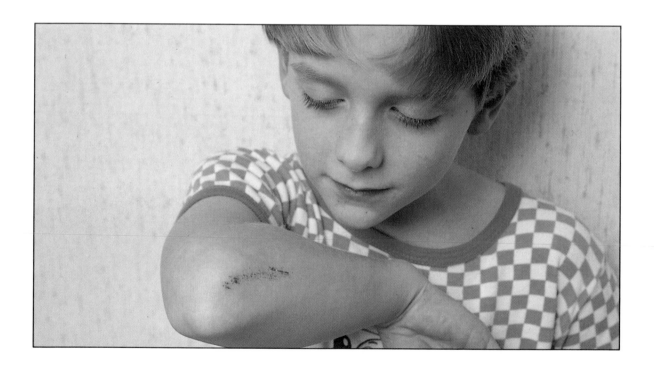

If you cut yourself, it is important that you clean the wound thoroughly. Wash off any bits of dirt, and bathe the cut with a **disinfectant** to kill off any germs. A big cut

14

may need a bandage. A deep cut will probably need to be stitched up by a doctor. Sometimes, stitches are a little painful, but they may be necessary to prevent infection and a bad scar.

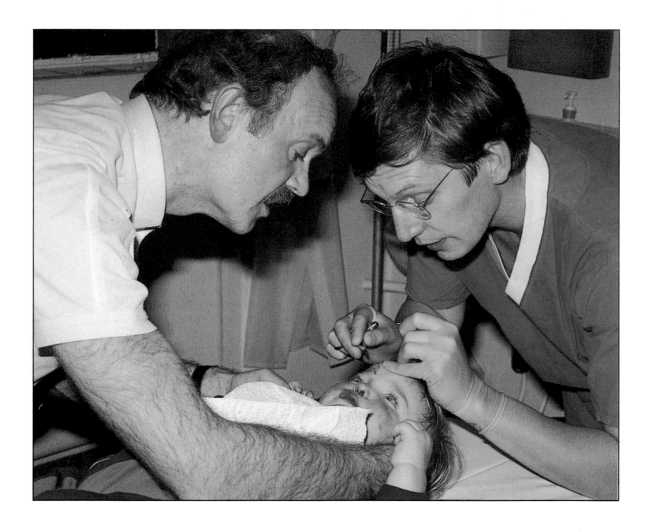

A bruise is like a cut, but it is inside your skin. It will be sore but will heal quite quickly.

Rashes on our skin

Many people have **allergic reactions**. These often cause rashes or blotches on the skin. Some people have allergic reactions to certain foods, like cheese or shellfish. Insect stings and bites can also cause irritating rashes and bumps.

If you suddenly notice a rash on your skin, show it to an adult because it might be serious. Usually a dab of

16

cream from a chemist will help stop your skin from itching, but sometimes you might need to see a doctor.

Have you ever been stung by a stinging nettle? Nettles can bring up a painful rash. Next time, see if there is a dock leaf nearby – it soothes the skin if you rub one over the nettle rash.

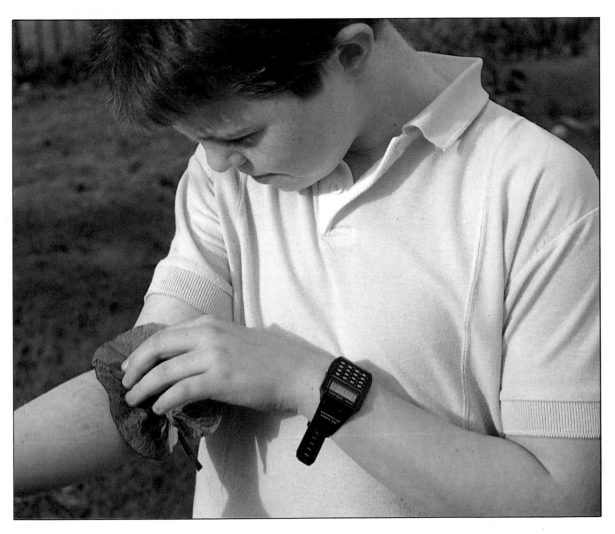

Spots and pimples

A blocked pore on your skin may develop into a spot. Regular washing should help prevent this happening.

Teenagers are especially troubled with spots because skin gets greasier at this age. This can lead to spots called **acne**. Greasy skin is a natural part of growing up.

Sunshine and a healthy diet can help prevent acne, and special ointments can help cure it.

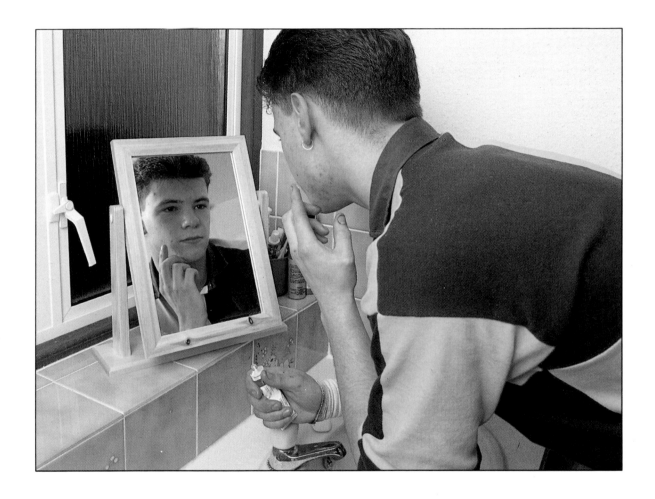

There are spotty illnesses too. Have you ever had chicken-pox or measles? If you have, you will know about spots and rashes, and how itchy your skin can feel. It is always best not to scratch spots. Your fingers may have germs on them that can make spots worse.

Marks on our skin

Freckles and moles are harmless patches of skin with an extra amount of **pigment** in them. This makes the skin darker. **Warts** are tiny, painless growths that can often be removed by the doctor if they bother you.

Birthmarks may be patches of skin with an extra large number of tiny blood vessels. They can also be caused by an extra amount of pigment.

Tattoos are pictures drawn in ink on the skin. It is not a good idea to have them because they are very difficult to remove. Many people with tattoos wish they had never had them done.

Sun and skin

Most people enjoy sunshine, but too much of it can be harmful. It dries out your skin and you can get sunburn.

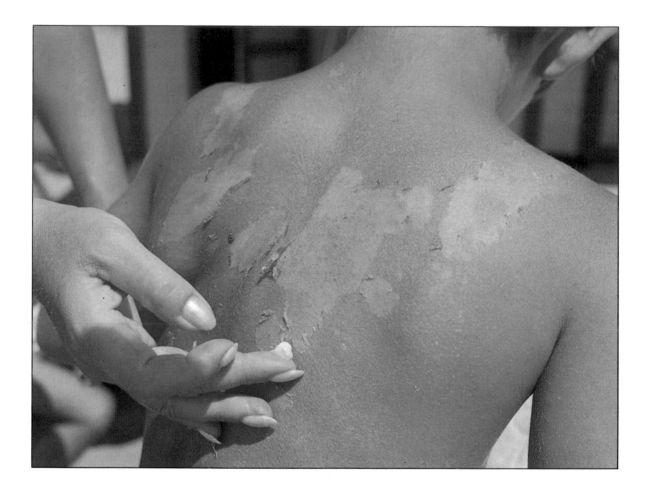

To prevent your skin being burned, use sun creams. You can buy these in different strengths, called **sun**

protection factors (SPFs). Start off with a strong one, such as SPF ten. Once your skin has got used to the sun, you can gradually use the weaker creams, such as SPF two or three.

Skiers can get sunburn because the snow reflects sunlight on to their faces. Skiers and windsurfers often wear sun block on their faces. This blocks out all of the sun's rays and gives extra protection.

Always remember that too much sun over a long period can cause serious illnesses such as skin **cancer**.

Cold weather and skin

Have you seen the faces of any deep-sea fishermen?
Their faces often look very weather-beaten. This is
because wind, rain and cold weather can be just as
harmful to your skin as sun.

24

It is important to wrap up well against the cold. In very cold parts of the world, people can even get **frost-bite**. Cold weather can cause **chapped** skin. You can stop your lips getting chapped by coating them with **lipsalve** before going out.

When you are cold, your body shivers. You also get little bumps all over your skin, called goose pimples. Shivering and goose pimples are a sign that you need warmer clothes.

Why people have different coloured skins

Everybody's skin contains a dark-coloured pigment called **melanin**. Black skin has a lot of melanin and white skin has a little. Melanin protects the skin from being burnt by the sun.

Millions of years ago, the people who lived in very hot, sunny countries – like India – developed a lot of melanin in their skins, to protect them from the sun. Their skins were black or brown. In colder countries,

26

where there was less sun, people needed less melanin in their skins for protection. These people had pale skins.

Nowadays, people travel around and choose to live in different countries. This means that people with different coloured skins often live together in the same country.

How age changes skin

When you are young your skin is very fresh, with a healthy colour. Your skin is firm, close-fitting and supple.

   As you get older this changes. Although your skin continues to produce new skin cells, they do not have the same 'sparkle'. The skin starts to sag, wrinkle and

28

grow paler. Wrinkles around the mouth and eyes are often called laugh lines. Have you ever noticed how your fingertips become white and crinkly after a long bath? Wrinkles are a bit like this.

Wrinkles cannot be prevented and they are a natural part of growing old. However, a healthy diet, regular washing and taking care of your skin in hot and cold weather will keep it at its best.

Glossary

Acne Bad spots that teenagers get.

Allergic reactions Rashes caused by something you are sensitive to.

Blood vessels Small tubes in the body through which blood flows.

Cancer A serious illness which can attack your skin.

Cells Tiny parts of every living plant and animal.

Chapped Cracked and rough skin, caused by cold weather.

Chlorine A chemical put in swimming-pools to kill germs.

Clot When blood thickens like jelly.

Disinfectant A liquid or cream that kills germs.

Flexible Able to bend easily.

Frost-bite Damage to the flesh – usually on the hands and feet – caused by freezing weather.

Infections Illnesses.

Lipsalve An ointment which can protect your lips in cold weather.

Melanin The part of your skin that keeps out the sun.

Nerve endings Sensitive parts of your body.

Pigment   A substance in your skin which gives it colour.

Pores   Tiny holes in the skin.

Rash   Blotches on the skin.

Sebum   An oily substance which makes your skin stretchy and waterproof.

Sun protection factors   The amount of protection given to the skin against the sun, by sun creams.

Vitamins   A number of substances found in small amounts in food, which are important for good health.

Warts   Hard lumps on the hands and face.

Wound   A scratch, or cut, on the skin.

Books to read

Body Facts by Dr Alan Maryon Davis (Macdonald, 1984).

Health and Hygiene by Dorothy Baldwin (Wayland, 1987).

Skin, Hair and Teeth by Bridget and Neil Ardley (Macmillan, 1989).

The Human Body Edited by Paulette Pratt (Hodder & Stoughton, 1984).

The Structure of Your Body by Dorothy Baldwin and Claire Lister (Wayland, 1983).

Picture acknowledgements

All photographs by Trevor Hill except *cover* Chris Fairclough; 6 Wayland; 21 Topham; 22 Zefa; 23 Richard and Sally Greenhill; 24 Cephas. Artwork by John Yates.

Index